WHEN THE FLOWER OPENS

The Extraordinary Friendship Between Abbot Shodo Habukawa and Monsignor Luigi Giussani

Mark Danner   **Joshua Stancil**

The image on our cover: *Thousand-Armed Chenresi*,
from 14th century Tibet
The painting in our logo: *Veil of Veronica*,
by Francisco de Zurbarán

*If a photo has no attribution, it means that after
reasonable attempts to track down the identity of the
photographer, his or her name remains unknown.*

*All images in this book were taken from the public
domain and are licensed under a Creative Commons
Attribution 4.0 International license.*

Main title font: Cinzel Decorative
Subtitle and body text font: Lora
Cover and layout design: Suzanne M. Lewis

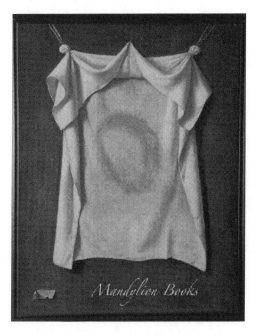

Mandylion Books

Monsignor Luigi Giussani

DEDICATION

For Servant of God Luigi Giussani, who followed.

CONTENTS

ACKNOWLEDGMENTS

The authors would like to thank all who gave of their time to this small book. A special thanks is reserved for Suzanne M. Lewis, whose patience saw this project through to completion.

Luigi Giussani and Shodo Habukawa at Koyasan in 1987

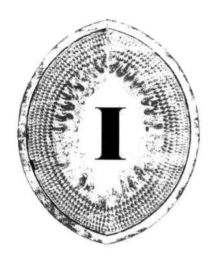

A MOST IMPROBABLE FRIENDSHIP

When the flower opens, the butterfly arrives; but, at the
same time, when the butterfly arrives, the flower opens.
— Japanese Proverb

Imagine:
In late August 2017 you find yourself on the eastern
coast of Italy, strolling the Rimini Fairgrounds, the
summer heat and Adriatic breeze in constant duel.
You're here for the Meeting of Friendship Among
Peoples (more commonly and simply known as "the
Meeting"), the largest week-long cultural event held
annually in Europe. A gesture of the Catholic ecclesial
movement Communion and Liberation, founded by
Monsignor Luigi Giussani, the Meeting offers a week of
exhibits, discussions, films, artistic displays, and
performances. Only yesterday you sat in the Arena

Spettacoli UnipolSai *for the China National Opera House's spellbinding performance of* Madame Butterfly. *The Meeting is an astounding swirl of people and cultures from around the globe.*

But now you check your watch: nearly three o'clock.

You walk into the Sala Illumia, intrigued by the title of the presentation about to begin: "From Which Heart Radiates a Thousand Hands: The Emerging Mystery of 30 Years of Friendship." What could be the meaning of such a title? Curious, you take a seat in the audience.

The stage is mostly bare, save for a long table across the center. Roberto Fontolan sits at the table, greets the audience and offers a few introductory remarks. He is soon joined by a Japanese woman, Makako Saito, who, to your surprise, speaks fluent Italian. Roberto describes her to the audience as "a woman at the linguistic crossroads of our worlds."

"I am very moved and happy," she says, "because thirty years of friendship is a beautiful thing that no one could even imagine. I must thank Don Giussani and Professor Habukawa, because they are two great masters. We will soon hear a prayer by Christians and Buddhists."

Father Giussani you've heard of; Professor Habukawa you haven't.

You hear a chime and see a group of Japanese Buddhist monks dressed in robes of bright purple and gold ascend the steps of the stage and form a line to the left of the table. One of the monks sets a chair in front of them, and then helps into the seat a bespectacled elderly monk clad in a bright orange robe. This is, you suddenly realize, the Professor Habukawa mentioned by Makako Saito: Shodo Habukawa, Abbot and Novice Master of the Buddhist monks of Mt. Koya, Japan.

A monk intones a solo prayer in Japanese and is soon joined by his brother monks. The chant begins low and rhythmic but then assumes an undulating force of its own, gently rising and falling like an ocean swell. The monks hold in their hands golden bowls filled with flower petals. Throughout their prayer, the monks scatter petals from their bowls as a kind of offering, a purification. Makako Saito explained this to the audience only moments ago: "When the Shingon monks offer a prayer, they throw flower petals. For us, this is the purification of the place: whoever manages to take one of these flower petals is a person loved by the Mystery. So, when the monks throw flowers, the one who finds them near is happier. And happiness is the purpose of life for everyone. Obviously, those who are unable to take the petals should not be sorry, for we are all embraced by the Mystery."

The chanting continues for nearly seven minutes, then pauses.

You suddenly become aware of another group onstage, to the right of the table. The Communion and Liberation (CL) choir, comprised of men and women, begin chanting an Alleluia. Your ears notice immediately the tonal difference between eastern and western musical traditions. And yet the plaintive, supplicant nature of the singing hints at an interior unity transcending geography and culture.

A pause.

Silence.

The monks take up again their low rhythmic chanting, almost metronomic in its purity, and are soon joined by the CL choir, whose voices come shimmering over the top of the chanting like the crest of a wave. You are transfixed by the otherworldly beauty of the mingling of tones, of voices. 'How is such beauty possible?' you wonder. And what does it mean?

3

The voices, tonally different yet harmonious, spiral upward, then surge and subside.

Silence.

The monks make their way off the stage, as do the CL choir members. Shodo Habukawa is helped to a seat at the table next to Roberto Fontolan. Makako Saito sits at Habukawa's side to translate.

At first, however, Habukawa needs no translator. He wants to show off his Italian skills.

"Buongiorno," he says, to the delight of the audience. "Buonasera," he continues. And then, showing his sense of humor: "Buon appetito!" You and the audience are charmed.

"My name is Shodo Habukawa Koyasan," he continues in Italian; then, switching to Japanese, "Many thanks for your dear invitation, again this year, to the Rimini Meeting. The encounter with the Mystery allows everyone to meet with the other, and meeting with the other helps us to deepen our experience."

Acknowledging the very real differences between Buddhists and Catholics, Habukawa nevertheless affirms that "despite the difference, we are united before the Mystery through prayer."

As he talks, you can't help but think back to the title of this presentation and wonder what it means. As if reading your mind, Habukawa explains.

"When Monsignor Luigi Giussani came to Mount Koya, he liked very much a Buddhist figure of Senjyu-kannon, a Buddhist deity of compassion depicted with a thousand arms holding different instruments and objects to help all those who suffer. I heard that, after returning to Italy, Don Giussani put a picture of Senjyu-kannon on his desk and never took it off. I will never forget his teaching and this episode."

How did the friendship between Father Giussani, an Italian priest and teacher, and Professor Habukawa, a Japanese Abbot, Novice Master, and University Professor, come about? And, furthermore, in the earthly absence of Father Giussani, who died in 2005, what has sustained the friendship between the Koyasan monks and the Movement of Communion and Liberation for over 30 years?

This book will offer a brief look at the improbable but very real friendship between Don Giussani and Professor Habukawa, and present it as the model of true ecumenism between believers in Jesus Christ and people of other cultures and faiths, people whose hearts beat with the same original needs as ours: for truth, beauty, and love. We will offer brief overviews of Christianity and Buddhism, and explore the development of friendships between members of Communion and Liberation and Buddhists of other countries and traditions.

This examination of an interfaith, multi-party friendship is, in itself, a journey in which we will seek and find much beauty, and as Fr. Giussani was fond of pointing out: when we seek beauty, we are seeking Christ.

GIUSSANI[1]

"We must be stimulated to personally confront our own origins."[2]
— *Luigi Giussani*

One of the most moving facts of Christian history is the great use God makes of meager vessels.

St. Paul, who admitted he was "unskilled in speaking,"[3] springs to mind, as do St. Francis of Assisi and St. Thérèse of Lisieux. In our own day, Servant of God Luigi Giussani provides a particularly striking

---

[1] This chapter offers a brief introduction to the life and thought of Monsignor Giussani. For those desiring more, the definitive treatment can be found in Alberto Savorana's monumental biography, *The Life of Luigi Giussani*, published by McGill-Queen's University Press.

[2] Luigi Giussani, *The Risk of Education* (New York: Crossroads Publishing Company, 2001), 67.

[3] 2 Corinthians 11:6, RSV.

example of this phenomenon. It is hard to imagine anyone predicting, seven decades ago at his ordination, the impact this diminutive priest would have on the Church and the world.

In 1922 he was born in Desio, a small town near Milan, Italy. His father, Beniamino, was an artist and a deeply committed Socialist. He instilled in young Luigi an abiding love of beauty—in poetry, in painting, and in music. He also imparted to his son a great desire for justice.

Luigi's mother, Angelina, was a woman of deep faith and religiosity, gifts she freely passed on to her son. In those days, boys entered the minor seminary very young, and Luigi began his studies at the diocesan seminary of Saint Peter Martyr Seveso at the tender age of ten. He would later often recount a seminal moment from those years:

> In my thoughts, in my memory, my mother has always been linked to the time—I was a seminarian still shedding my first tears of homesickness—I went home for Easter...There was a beautiful sky and the air was so clear, and there was only one last star in the sky, the morning star. As we walked in the wind—there was a high wind—toward the priest's house, my mother spoke these words, "What a beautiful world, and how great God is!" quite simply, like people say, "Milk porridge is very nice." [...] But there's a world of difference between the way my mother said it and the way we can repeat this phrase. This world of difference can be summed up in one thing: that what my mother said is true, truly human, and anyone who does not say it is not human. What made my mother so sensitive was not a special

7

brain or a particularly oversized heart; it was a gift of the Spirit."[4]

A moment such as this does not serve as an exercise in sentimentality; it provides a concrete witness to the truth of things. The very concreteness of his mother's statements would radically—in the truest sense of the word—affect Giussani's understanding of the Catholic faith. *Witness*, he would come to understand, constitutes a way of sharing a fact. And Christianity is shared through an encounter with a witness:

> *Those two, John and Andrew, those twelve, Simon and the others, told their wives, and some of their wives joined them. At a certain point, many women joined them and followed: they left their homes behind and went with them. They told other friends, who did not necessarily abandon their homes, but who shared in their fondness, in their favorable and wonder-filled disposition towards that Man, and shared their faith in Him. And those friends told other friends, then other friends, then even more friends. The first century went by in this way, and these friends flooded the second century as well as the known world with their faith. They reached Spain by the end of the first century and India by the second century. Then those people of the second century told others who lived after them, and those people told others who came after them. Like a growing stream and then a river that grew and grew, these people told my*

---

[4] *Dal Temperamento un Metodo* [From Temperament a Method] (Milan: BUR, 2002), 357.

mother, my mom. And my mom told me, when I was little.[5]

As Pope Benedict XVI would later note in the opening encyclical of his pontificate (echoing the thought of Giussani), "Being Christian is not the result of an ethical choice or a lofty idea, but the encounter with an event, a person, which gives life a new horizon and a decisive direction."[6]

This insight, which young Giussani gleaned from his mother, became the axis around which his entire understanding of Christianity spun. Christianity is not primarily a moralism, Giussani taught, the slavish adherence to a list of Dos and Don'ts; rather it is an intimate relationship with a Fact. Giussani would later stress that the human person is not *in a relationship with God*, but that the person, by virtue of being the fruit of a creative and divine love, *is relationship with God.*

Giussani asserts that the evidence for this fact lies, perhaps surprisingly, within the human heart. Its original needs—for truth, for beauty, to love and be loved—are universal and demand a total answer. We are not happy with half-measures. We disdain delays. We are not satisfied with a temporary or partial happiness—our hearts beat for something totalizing and infinite. And it is precisely here where we experience the greatest frustration: our desires are infinite, yet our abilities—and indeed the vast galaxies swirling around us—are finite. Man "lives on this earth and is committed to a temporal destiny; yet there is in him something that goes beyond any terrestrial

---

[5] Quoted in Alberto Savorana, *The Life of Luigi Giussani* (Montreal: McGill-Queen's University Press, 2018), 397.

[6] Benedict XVI, *Deus caritas est* [God is love], vatican.va, 1.

horizon and seeks the atmosphere of eternity as its natural climate."[7] What, then, can fulfill this longing?

For Giussani and the Christian tradition, Jesus of Nazareth proposes Himself as the totalizing answer to these questions–the infinite fulfilment of our infinite desire. He does this not by proposing a text or a work, but instead by proposing Himself.

The Tenth Hour

Giussani cherished the fourth Gospel's narrative of John and Andrew's first encounter with Jesus. It may well be the Gospel passage he recounted and explicated more often than any other, for he saw within it the fundamental element of Christianity: an encounter with an exceptional presence:

> *What does "exceptional" mean? When can something be defined as "exceptional"? When it corresponds adequately to the heart's original expectations, however confused and hazy one's awareness of it may be. Exceptional is, paradoxically, when what is most "natural" for us appears. And what is "natural" for us? That what we desire should come true. For nothing is more natural than the satisfaction of the ultimate and profound desire of our heart, nothing is more natural than the answer to the needs that lie at the root of our being, those needs for which we actually live and move.*
>
> *Our heart has an ultimate, imperious, deep-set need for fulfillment, for truth, beauty, goodness, love, final certitude, and happiness. So to come*

---

[7] Henri De Lubac, *The Splendor of the Church* (New York: Sheed and Ward, 1956), 166.

across an answer to these needs should be the most obvious and normal thing. Yet, on the contrary, this correspondence, which should be supremely normal, becomes supremely exceptional for us. To come face-to-face with something absolutely and profoundly natural, that is to say, something that corresponds to the needs of the heart that nature gives us, is therefore something absolutely exceptional. There is, as it were, a strange contradiction: what normally happens is never truly exceptional, because it does not respond adequately to the needs of our heart.

It is the exceptionality of the figure of Christ, then, that makes it easy to recognize Him. For John and Andrew, that Man corresponded to the irresistible and undeniable needs of their heart in a way that was unimaginable. There was no one like that Man. In the encounter with Him, they felt an unimagined, unimaginable correspondence to the heart that they had never before experienced. What an unprecedented astonishment He must have awoken in the two who first met Him, and later in Simon, Philip, and Nathanael![8]

If Christ, the incarnation of God, embodies the fulfillment of man's infinite desire, how can people living today, some two thousand years later, experience the same encounter, the same fulfillment? Aren't we lacking the astonishing correspondence that Christ's first disciples experienced?

In fact, the people of today can and do meet Christ, through the Church, which is the physical prolongation of His presence in human history. As Giussani intuited from his mother, the faith has reached us, two millennia later, via a vast series of

---

[8] Quoted in *Magnificat*, www.aleteia.org/daily-prayer/thursday-november-30/daily-meditation-1/.

human encounters that began on a dusty path in Bethany, when John and Andrew met an exceptional Presence who, instead of asking, "What have you done?" asked, "What are you looking for?"

The Risk of Educating

In 1945, near the close of World War II, Giussani was ordained to the priesthood at the surprisingly young age of twenty-three. His path to ordination had been accelerated by the authorities in the Milan archdiocese, because they feared his serious respiratory health problems, which would plague him the rest of his life, would lead to his death before he could receive the sacrament of Holy Orders.

Following ordination, Giussani took a teaching post at the Venegono Seminary. His academic interests were American Protestantism and Eastern Christian theology.

Despite his promising career in the seminary, in 1954, he abruptly asked his superiors for permission to leave his position to pursue high school teaching. His request had been provoked by an unsettling experience during a train ride, in which he met some young people: "During a vacation train trip to the Adriatic Sea, I started a conversation with some high school students—and found them shockingly ignorant of the Church and Church teachings. I had to assume that their ignorance was caused by complete indifference toward, and in some cases even disgust with, the Church. At that point, I decided to devote my life to restoring a Christian presence at the high school level."[9]

---

[9] Quoted in Antonio Gaspari, "Communion and Liberation," *Inside the Vatican.* February 1996.

12

He began teaching at the Berchet high school in Milan, where he remained until the 1960s. Not long after arriving at Berchet, however, something pivotal happened:

> One day, returning from work and ruminating on [the] incapacity of Christianity to inspire youth, I encountered four boys discussing animatedly together. I asked if they were Christians, and they answered "yes," but a bit uneasily. Then I continued. "You say you are Christians, but in the school assemblies, only the Communists and Fascist-Monarchists debate together. Where are the Christians?" The next week these four initiated a debate in the school assembly, introducing themselves as "we Catholics." From that moment and for the next ten years, Christianity and the Church were the most heatedly debated topics in school meetings.[10]

Under Giussani's leadership, the *Gioventù Studentesca* (shortened to GS), or "student youth," enabled Catholic students to become protagonists in the school alongside the communist and secular groups.

The Movement of Communion and Liberation grew from this experience. Students who had graduated high school and had begun their university studies missed the exceptional presence of that small Milanese priest and sought him out, asking if there were some way to continue their friendship and deepen the experience of what they had encountered. From this sprang the CLU (members of Communion and Liberation attending university), the Fraternity of Communion and Liberation, and eventually *Memores Domini*, an association of consecrated lay people who

---

[10] *Ibid.*

live communally in the world. More recently, the charism of Father Giussani has generated two religious orders, the Priestly Fraternity of St. Charles Borromeo and the Sisters of Charity of the Assumption, as well as a lay association, the Fraternity of St. Joseph.

Communion and Liberation is now present in over 80 countries and numbers some 100,000 followers. Gestures inspired by the experience of CL include the Rimini Meeting, the New York Encounter, the Festival of Friendship, and the annual "Tents" food drive in Italy.

All these fruits sprang from a gift to an unpretentious young priest whose frail health, it was feared, would overtake him before his ordination and who had not planned to found anything.

In a 2004 letter to Pope John Paul II, marking the Movement's fiftieth anniversary, Giussani wrote:

> Not only did I have no intention of "founding" anything, but I believe that the genius of the Movement that I saw coming to birth lies in having felt the urgency to proclaim the need to return to the elementary aspects of Christianity, that is to say, the passion of the Christian fact as such in its original elements, and nothing more. Perhaps it was precisely this that awoke the unforeseeable possibility of encounter with personalities of the Jewish, Muslim, Buddhist, Protestant and Orthodox worlds, from the United States to Russia, in an impetus of embrace and an appreciation of all that remains of truth, of beauty, of good and of right in whoever lives a sense of belonging.[11]

---

[11] Luigi Giussani, "Letter sent by Fr Giussani to John Paul II on the 50th Anniversary of the birth of Communion and Liberation," *Traces*, no. 4, 2004, 1–3.

For Monsignor Giussani, the certainty of the Christian fact enables an unparalleled openness toward one's fellow human beings, for through the Incarnation, God has united Himself in a mysterious way with every person.

BUDDHISM AND CHRISTIANITY

"This body needs no opening to the world; it is itself the opening that God has created for Himself in order to enter into the world's material and historical reality, its destiny and becoming."[12]
— Hans Urs Von Balthasar

Although an exhaustive treatment of Christian and Buddhist beliefs lies far beyond the scope of this slim volume, it will be helpful nevertheless to offer a brief overview of each faith's distinctive features. Much of modern ecumenism stresses similarities and points of agreement; this is not, in itself, a bad thing. Christianity and Buddhism, for example, do indeed share many similarities, particularly in their monastic

---

[12] Hans Urs Von Balthasar, *Truth is Symphonic* (San Francisco: Ignatius Press, 1987), 93.

traditions. The reality of the rather sizable differences between the faiths, however, makes the 1987 encounter between Luigi Giussani and Shodo Habukawa—as well as the friendship that blossomed between Communion and Liberation and the Koyasan monks—so very surprising and precious.

We'll begin by turning toward Asia.

Offering a concise overview of Buddhism presents a considerable challenge, for it is a strikingly diverse religion. Many in the West assume, incorrectly, that there exists a single homogenous entity known as Buddhism, founded by a seeker of enlightenment who boasted a pleasantly cherubic belly. The reality proves quite different, and notably difficult to synopsize.

In its variety of schools and strains, Buddhism resembles Protestant Christianity, which is similarly difficult to encapsulate. Just as no one can point to a single "official" form of Protestantism, no single "official" form of Buddhism typifies them all. What follows, then, offers a necessarily broad overview of the religion as a whole.

Buddhism

Siddhãrtha Gautama, the founder of Buddhism, a Hindu prince who also carried the name Sakyamuni (sage of Sakya clan), was born in northern India sometime in the sixth century B.C., and led, not surprisingly for a prince, a rather lavish and pampered life. He began to roam, however, and witnessed the sufferings of those outside his world.[13] Deeply troubled by the unending misery he observed,

---

[13] One tradition holds that he came upon three examples of suffering: an ascetic, a sick man, and a corpse.

at age twenty-nine he abandoned his wife, children, and palace to seek out the meaning of, and solution to, human suffering.

He initially pursued an alarmingly severe asceticism but eventually abandoned this effort in favor of meditation. One day during his thirty-fifth year, while meditating in the shade of a bodhi tree, Siddhãrtha achieved a spiritual breakthrough that helped him identify certain truths about life and death, reincarnation, karma, and suffering. He concluded that he had to rid himself of spiritual defilements, which he recognized as desire, hate, and delusion. Moreover, he sought the eradication of cravings, even those of hunger and thirst. He identified this breakthrough beneath the bodhi tree as a moment of enlightenment and consequently assumed the title of Buddha, which means "the enlightened one." He described his newfound deliverance from desire as a state of "being blown out" (as an oil lamp) or "quenched," that is, *nirvana*, the point at which a person escapes from the cycle of life, suffering, death, and reincarnation.

The Four Noble Truths The Buddha's moment of enlightenment beneath the bodhi tree revealed to him what he called the Four Noble Truths: 1. life is suffering; 2. suffering is the result of desires or attachments; 3. freeing oneself from desires and attachments will end suffering; 4. the way to achieve nirvana involves adhering to the Eight-fold Path.

The Four Noble Truths relate closely to one another and follow a certain logic. The first one identifies the problem: *life is suffering*. The second identifies the source of the problem: *desires and attachments*. The third offers a solution to the problem: *divesting oneself from all desires and attachments*. And the fourth provides the mechanism whereby one can succeed in fulfilling the Third Noble Truth: *adherence to the Eight-fold Path*.

The Eight-fold Path The Eight-fold Path can be divided into three sections, the first of which relates to wisdom (or *prajñā*) and consists of *Right View*, to see the world–including the reality of karma and suffering–from a Buddhist perspective, and *Right Intention*, the resolve to rid oneself of any illicit desire.

In the second section of the Eight-fold Path, Buddhists guard against outward actions that can defile their minds. This section concerns itself with ethics (or *śīla*) and exhorts followers to practice *Right Speech*, in which they watch their words to avoid lying, any form of verbal abuse, or spreading gossip and slander; *Right Action*, which enjoins them to behave in a morally upright fashion, neither harming nor corrupting others; and *Right Livelihood*, which prohibits Buddhists from engaging in occupations and trades that harm other living beings, either directly or indirectly.

The third and final section of the Eight-fold Path concerns itself with unified mind (or *samādhi*) and teaches Buddhists to cultivate *Right Effort*, by continually striving, through an act of will that involves ongoing moral effort, to rid themselves of words and actions that are harmful to themselves or others; *Right Mindfulness*, which encourages them to remain continuously mentally alert and sensitive to what may be influencing their minds and bodies and to be intentional and deliberate about saying and doing what is morally right; and *Unified Mind*, which calls the Buddhist to engage in the practice of regular meditation, in order to enter into *jhana*, a state of consciousness that allows the believer to develop wisdom and insight.

Because Buddhism teaches that suffering is a result of craving, following the Eight-fold Path promises adherents the possibility to attain *nirvana*, the cessation of desire.

Development and Spread of the Faith Buddhism flourished as a monastic movement in India, but waned over time as it was overshadowed by Hinduism and, much later, by Islam. It spread south to Sri Lanka and east throughout Asia. Over time, two major schools emerged:

1. *Theravada*: Theravada Buddhism abounds in Southeast Asia, especially in Thailand, Myanmar, Cambodia, and Laos. Historically, to achieve *nirvana* in this branch of Buddhism requires a high level of personal commitment and therefore, monks and nuns have emerged as the exemplary practitioners of Buddhism in these countries.

2. *Mahayana*: Mahayana Buddhism prevails in Sri Lanka, Japan, Taiwan, China, Korea, Vietnam, and Tibet. This branch represents the form of the faith that Westerners often have in mind when they think of Buddhism. In this form of Buddhism, everyone, including lay people, can practice the faith, without need for example or mediation, to achieve enlightenment.

Traditionally, Buddhism has had no concept of a creator God. While not expressly forbidding such a belief, most strains of Buddhism find it irrelevant to the goal of the believer, which is to achieve *nirvana*, enlightenment. Here we glimpse the great openness of Shodo Habukawa and his monks, who do not hesitate to speak of the Mystery, the title by which Fr. Giussani often referred to God, creator of all things.

Christianity

The history of Christianity is no less complex than that of Buddhism, and providing a comprehensive

overview of the religion's three main branches—
Catholic, Protestant, and Orthodox—would require
multiple volumes. For our purposes here we will
concentrate primarily on the tradition that nurtured
Fr. Giussani, Catholic Christianity.

According to Christian teaching, God chose a
people, the Hebrews, with which to identify Himself.
He tasks them with "spread[ing] the knowledge of His
Mystery throughout the world and in all times, 'in all
nations.'"[14] Over the course of centuries, the Hebrews
committed their history and beliefs to an
authoritative text, the *Tanakh*. A prominent feature of
this text is the longing for, and indeed a prophecy of,
a coming Messiah (or Christ), a man born of a virgin
and anointed by God to deliver the Jewish people
from their suffering.

Two thousand years ago, a Jewish man named
Jesus, from the small town of Nazareth, claimed to be
the longed-for messiah. He chose twelve apostles,
who followed Him for approximately three years. His
exceptionality attracted a broader group of followers,
male and female, who were moved by His teachings
and by His gentleness and lack of scandal at their
sinfulness. But by identifying Himself with the
outcasts of society—the poor, the lapsed, the ritually
unclean—Jesus ran afoul of Jewish religious
authorities, who considered blasphemous His claims
of divinity and took exception to what appeared to be
His superseding of the religious laws laid down in the
Tanakh. Roman authorities, meanwhile, feared His
growing popularity could trigger an insurrection
against Imperial rule in Judea and Israel. Events came
to a head.

Judas, one of Jesus' twelve disciples, betrayed His
location to Roman authorities, who arrested Jesus at
night in the Garden of Gethsemane. Beaten, scourged,

---

[14] Luigi Giussani, "We Are Jews," *Traces*, No. 1, 1999.

and mockingly crowned with thorns by Roman soldiers, Jesus was then taken outside Jerusalem's city walls to Golgotha, a hill on which the Roman's routinely executed criminals. There, between two other convicted men, Jesus was cruelly nailed to a cross in front of onlookers, who included His mother, Mary, and His young disciple, John.[15]

Approximately three hours later, Jesus died and was taken down from the cross and given to His mother.[16]

His followers, chief among them Mary Magdalene, prepared His body for burial and placed His body in a tomb sealed by a large stone.

Three days later, early on a Sunday morning, Mary Magdalene returned to the tomb and discovered that the stone had been rolled away and the tomb now sat empty. Jesus then appeared to her—not as a phantom or spirit but rather in the flesh—and asked her to tell the other disciples of His resurrection. She did as asked, but the disciples refused to believe her. Two of them, Peter (the head of the apostles) and John, decided to visit the tomb themselves. When they discovered that Mary had been telling the truth, they raced back to Jerusalem and quickly spread the word that Jesus had risen.

Over the next forty days, Jesus appeared many times to His followers, talking with them, eating with them, reassuring them that once He departed, He would send the Holy Spirit to guide and comfort them.

He ascended to heaven in front of His followers, and ten days later, as promised, the Holy Spirit descended upon a small group of followers gathered

---

[15] John distinguished himself as the only disciple not to flee following Jesus' arrest in Gethsemane.

[16] Michelangelo's sculpture, *Pietà*, is one of the most popular representations of this event.

around His mother, Mary. From there, the small group of followers began spreading the "good news," or *Gospel*, of Jesus' sacrificial atonement for the sins of mankind. Jesus, His disciples and apostles taught, was the longed-for Christ who had indeed liberated people from oppression—the oppression of sin. People who accepted Jesus as Messiah were now freed to be their authentic selves.

"In the Mystery of the Resurrection," Fr. Giussani once said, "lies the summit and the highest intensity of our Christian self-awareness, and therefore that of my new awareness of myself, of the way in which I look at all people and all things. The key to the novelty in the relationship between me and myself, between me and others, between me and things is in the Resurrection."[17]

Growth The Christian community began small but grew rapidly. The most important convert of early Christianity was Paul of Tarsus, who spread the faith with an unmatched zeal, planting Christian communities throughout the Mediterranean world. Over the following decades, the writings of Paul began to circulate and assume the status of scripture. These writings were soon joined by others, including narratives of Jesus' life, and eventually a collection of Christian scriptures took shape. The *Tanakh* came to be called the *Old Testament*, with the Christian writings named the *New Testament*. Christians accepted both as sacred.

In the fourth century, the Roman Emperor Constantine converted to Christianity and lifted all restrictions on what had until then been a persecuted minority. Although not designated the official state religion—a development still decades away—Christianity benefited greatly from Constantine's

---

[17] Luigi Giussani, "The Risen Christ: the Defeat of Nothingness," *Traces*, No. 4, 1996.

23

conversion, and quickly gained adherents. In a relatively short amount of time, Christianity swept the Roman Empire.

Distinctive Beliefs Christianity proposes Jesus of Nazareth as the Messiah prophesied in the Old Testament, and as the virgin-born incarnation of God. Because men and women cannot hope to completely atone for their sins, Jesus—God in the flesh—offered Himself on the cross as a sacrificial atonement. Christ's bodily resurrection indicates the intrinsic value of the flesh, of matter. In the end, Christianity declares that Jesus saves the whole person, body and soul.

Following scripture and tradition, the Catholic Church recognizes the Bishop of Rome as the successor of Peter and thus head of the Church on earth.

Both Buddhism and Christianity share a love of creation. Alongside its call for detachment from all things, Buddhism demonstrates an obvious appreciation of and care for nature. Buddhist art, for example, revels in depictions of trees, flowers, butterflies, and birds. Meanwhile summer does not officially begin in Japan until people can hear the whir of cicadas.

Christians also appreciate nature, seeing in everything a sign of nature's Creator. Christianity affirms the goodness of matter, and ascribes great importance, for example, to the particular places Jesus visited during His earthly sojourn.

More specifically, in Christian worship, Catholics venerate relics and icons, anoint themselves and others with blessed water, and make pilgrimages to holy sites.

Buddhists and Christians are sensitive to human suffering, and work diligently to alleviate it wherever and whenever possible, especially through acts of charity and self-sacrifice. In Shingon Buddhism, perhaps more than in most other forms of the faith, everything speaks of an aspiration for the Absolute.

For Christians, God became incarnate precisely to bridge this chasm between the Absolute and man.

Perhaps the most noticeable difference between Buddhism and Christianity concerns the notion of the person. In Buddhism, the goal is to recognize one's personhood as essentially "egoless" and as subsumed by the whole of reality, as illustrated in a poem by Shingon Buddhism's founder, Kukai:

All Beings as individuals are appearances only, like illusions:
They are composites of forever changing constituents.
Our blind desires, which are neither within nor without,
With their ensuing actions, delude us more and more.

The world is at once the creating and the created;
It is the Lotus Realm, the Infinite continuum of Reality.
Neither empty nor non-empty, nor the oneness of the two,
It is void, temporal, and yet real, beyond name and form...[18]

In Christianity, meanwhile, the human person is the crowning pinnacle and whole reason for creation:

> *A fundamental factor of Jesus' outlook is the existence in man of a reality far superior to any other reality subject to time and space. The whole world is not as worthy as the most insignificant*

---

[18] From a letter that Kukai sent to a friend (quoted in *Kukai: Major Works* (New York: Columbia University Press, 1972), 80.

human person. Nothing in the universe can compare with a person, from the first instant of his conception until the last step of his decrepit old age.[19]

This Christian emphasis on the value of the human generates a fascination in the believer, a recognition that the other—who may look and sound very different, who may be of a different faith or no faith at all—is a good for the believer, and in some sense given to the believer by Christ Himself.

Fr. Giussani always insisted that the human heart's original needs—for beauty, for truth, for justice, and for love—are universal and found in every man and woman. In his encounter with Shodo Habukawa and the Koyasan monks, the subject to which we now turn, this faith in the human heart was richly rewarded, and became the occasion for a journey that has not, even thirty years later, reached its conclusion.

---

[19] Luigi Giussani, *At the Origin of the Christian Claim* (Montreal: McGill-Queen's University Press, 1998), 84.

Professor Habukawa and the Monks of Koyasan at the Rimini Meeting

Professor Habukawa at the Rimini Meeting

Professor Habukawa with a Portrait of Father Giussani (© Salvatori)

Professor Habukawa Prays at Father Giussani's Grave

THE ENCOUNTER AT MT. KOYA

"Only someone who is silent is listening."[20]
— Joseph Pieper

Neither man said a word.

Seconds ticked by. Fr. Giussani remained silent, as did Professor Shodo Habukawa, Novice Master of the Mt. Koya monks. They gazed intently at one another, then embraced.

The Italian priest had spent the morning traveling by train and cable car to this place, Koyasan, the monastery of Mt. Koya and center of Shingon Buddhism. Roberto Fontolan, a member of the small group that accompanied Fr. Giussani from Italy, described in his diary the otherworldly magnificence

---

[20] Josef Pieper, *A Brief Reader on the Virtues of the Human Heart* (San Francisco: Ignatius Press, 1991), 12.

into which they had just stepped: "You open the door and you're in 1600. Gorgeous. Everything in wood, painted dividers made of paper, bamboo, basins to wash in a sort of common bath. A sprawling, manicured garden and, beyond it, the tree-covered hills."[21]

Their embrace lingered in silence for several minutes.

Twenty years later, when asked about the encounter, Professor Habukawa said, "In this life, I will never forget that remarkable day, June 28, 1987, at one o'clock, when Monsignor Luigi Giussani appeared in front of my eyes in a dazzling clear light, the characteristic light of the beginning of summer. For a little time, we embraced each other in silence; no word was needed. The strong emotion of this first encounter has remained unforgettable."[22]

No word was needed. Professor Habukawa was a Novice Master, and as such possessed a keen insight into human nature. He immediately recognized in Fr. Giussani a fellow master of the religious life, a recognition returned by the Italian priest. Pavel Florenskij, the great Russian Orthodox theologian, once wrote that "the mystical unity of two is a condition of knowledge and the manifestation of the Spirit of Truth, who grants this knowledge."[23] Monsignor Giussani and Professor Habukawa experienced this unity in a profound and surprising way, forging an immediate bond centered on the human heart and not merely on words.

---

[21] Quoted in Savorana, *The Life of Luigi Giussani*, 739.

[22] Quoted in *Traces*, No. 6, 2007.

[23] Pavel Forenskij, *La Colonna e il fondamento della verità* [The Pillar and Foundation of Truth] (Milan: Rusconi, 1974), 495.

Nagoya

*The day before his encounter with Habukawa, Giussani
had addressed a large gathering in Nagoya, the largest
city in the Chūbu region of Japan. He had been invited
by the mayor to give a conference as part of a week-
long celebration of Italy sponsored by Nagoya's
International Cultural Center.*

*Fr. Giussani's remarks, given after a Japanese
choir's surprise performance of Povera Voce, a song of
the Communion and Liberation, offer a tremendous
insight into his understanding of religiosity and the
human heart, and help one better understand the
immediacy of his affection for Professor Habukawa.
They are presented here in full:*

A Unity of Human Existence
by Luigi Giussani

I am most honored to be among you, who represent
one of the greatest, most active, and most courteous
peoples of the world.

I must ask forgiveness of you all, and of those in
charge of the International Center, for having come
to speak to you here without a sound knowledge of
your history and without being able to speak
Japanese; but I accepted, so I begin.

I am putting great trust in your humanity, too,
because I am entrusting thoughts and feelings that
are dear to me to a translation that must not be easy,
and I am sorry not to be able to establish a direct
dialogue with you. I hope that all this does not
prevent that human communication, which I cordially
thank you for having given me the opportunity to
have with you.

I express my thanks, too, for the surprise offered
by the choir, because what they have sung is the first
song created by the Movement of my friends more

than thirty years ago; this song summarizes all the passion of our activity: to help all those we meet to be positive in life, in the meaning of life. Our voice sings with a reason, our life has a meaning.

Today I would like to bear witness to this fact, rather than give a talk.

However foreign our origins may be from the geographical and even historical point of view, no distance, no difference can create a total foreignness between us: we are all human.

Between us there is a unity of human existence. The expression 'human existence' implies a knowledge and a judgment, a use, an enjoyment of reality and of the world, but above all a common destiny. So I'll take the liberty of not reading, but saying instead what I feel in my heart, because I am deeply moved by your humanity. The first thing that strikes one, on looking at the skies, and the earth, and everything, is that no person is isolated. Existence in isolation cannot be conceived: one can imagine something on its own, but cannot encounter the existence of something on its own. From the little I know of your cultural history, this seems to be a value that your people feel very much. I am speaking of that total harmony, that unity amongst all things, thanks to which it is possible for all things to live. It is one of the most acute aspects of the sensitivity of your culture. As in this poem, by Matsuo Bashō, your culture exhibits a sensitivity that we don't find elsewhere: 'Flowers from an unknown tree filled my soul with their fragrance.'[24]

It is impossible to find a more perfect expression of the nexus between all things, even those which are yet unknown. But this great and total harmony, this unity amongst all things, also seems to have a mysterious meaning for my [individual] life. I don't

---

[24] English translator unknown.

know what all this sea means for my little drop. The spiritual tradition in which I grew told me that this great and mysterious harmony has a voice. This is the most important point of human thought, because my relationship with this total harmony is my destiny. This whole, this harmony, has a voice: what is it? It is a voice that is the same for me, for a Japanese, for a person of twenty million years ago, for someone a million centuries in the future: it's the same.

When a woman brings a child into the world, she gives it a structure by which you understand it is a human being. Every person that is born from a woman's womb has a face, which reflects this same interior structure. This is why I felt at home thanks to the kindness of the hostess, Anarita of Tokyo, and at the International Center of Nagoya. This is why I feel like speaking; I dare to speak to you.

The Voice of the Heart of Humanity The voice of the universe—of the 'all' of which we are a small, infinitesimal part—this voice is [also lodged in] the heart of humanity. When we look at the stars or the sea, when we fall in love with a woman, when we look tenderly at our children, when we strive to know nature and to use it, people of all ages, of all races, are searching for happiness: what is true, what is just, what is beautiful. Our ancient philosophers used to say: 'Search for being.' Whatever we see in the universe, in reality, arouses our desire for beauty, for goodness, for justice, for happiness. This is the voice that the universe, the whole, realizes: it is called the human heart.

So the great cultural and existential alternative is clear: either this voice has no meaning, is not real, and the human heart does not exist, or everything has a meaning for the human heart. Our voice sings with a reason, and our struggle, if you can call it that, is for awakening and sustaining in ourselves the sense of the ultimate positivity of life and of the heart. It is for

33

this ultimate relationship, this ultimate destiny for happiness that we live, whether consciously or not. It is for this ultimate desire for a real justice that we can endure today's toil. Without this hypothesis it would be unjust to give birth to children.

It is evident for everyone that conscious life is inconceivable if not in function of a value, that is to say, a destiny that is for one's existence, for one's heart, one's desires. All the rest is secondary to the happiness the heart desires, because marriage can work out well, it can be lucky, but it has its limit and even those who are most deeply in love can end up with the terrible temptations of boredom or disillusion. Even the greatest feelings, even those more humanly pleasing, can end up in banality and cynicism. And who is there who doesn't know the sadness of the precarious nature of the good of the people, or the good of the nation? Because everything is so dependent on unforeseeable factors and what we belong to is a great enigma, so that work is welcome, because it doesn't leave us too much time for thinking!

"What About Me and My Heart?" But a person may ask, 'Why do I work?' and the reply will be a social one. But 'What about me and my heart?' This is why a person I honor, Jesus, said, 'What use is it if you get all you want and lose the meaning of yourself?' or, 'What can man give in exchange for his own life?' I believe that the greatest things in our life are our values. But what is a value? A value is the link, the relationship, between my person, committed within life through an action, and my destiny. However this relationship with destiny in the things I do may be conceived, this is what gives life dignity. The awareness of this relationship has two advantages. First of all it is useful for the equilibrium of society, because it provides the sense of unity among all; and, secondly, it does not favor society to the detriment of one's person, in a forgetfulness of one's person, in the breakdown of the person.

I believe there is nothing in my education that I must testify to more strongly than this inexorable feeling, this irreducible feeling for my 'I,' for my person. The greater this sense of my own dignity, the more I will seek to serve others, to serve society. But the whole life of society exists for the person, for me, so that I may walk toward my destiny. ... I am relationship with the infinite, with the eternal, with everything. I use the word, "person," a great word of my tradition, not "humanity," defined abstractly, as by Marx or Feuerbach, but the person, in whom beats the heart given him by his mother. I believe that all my emotion and the fact that I'm moved by my Christian tradition are due to this discovery that it had me make of the human person, of the value of the individual, in whom lies the root and foundation of a social peace, of a peace amongst all.

A Passion for Every Man and Woman Allow me a reminiscence: the first time I went to South America, twenty-five years ago, I arrived there on a huge ship, [which brought us] a thousand kilometers up the Amazon River to the region called Macapá, which was all impenetrable forest; there were no roads, so you had to travel everywhere by boat or cross immense swamps. In such a huge territory there were about seventy thousand people, and many of them were called *Sirianos*. They live alone in the virgin rainforest for months on end, in continuous danger of death, and I never saw one of them smile. There is a group of priests who are friends of mine and they divide up the territory and for twenty or forty days they move around visiting, even going to find the most distant *Siriano*. One afternoon one of these friends of mine was due to set off on this terrible trip and he said to me, 'Come with me,' and immediately I answered yes. As the dusk came, we reached the edge of the swamp and he put on his wading boots and he said to me, laughing, 'Now stop here and go back,' and I stopped, and for the rest of my life I will remember that evening as the sun went down in ten minutes at the equator, in ten minutes you pass from sunshine to darkness and I saw that tall man walking away, and every so often he would turn around and wave to me while laughing. I was there rigid, looking at him and saying to myself, 'This man risks his life in order to go and find another man that he may never see again!' He was risking his life for *a* person. In that moment I understood what Christianity is: a passion for the person, a love for each and every person. Not for the "mankind" of the liberal-Marxist philosophers, a product of their own thinking, but for the person that you are, that I am.

And as the meaning of nature cannot be me, alone, so small and fleeting, the meaning of the whole of nature is rather my relationship with the infinite, my relationship with the Mystery that makes all things.

Tradition Illumines the Desires of the Heart But now I would like to say some things to move toward the end of my testimony. Another writer of your literature, the Emperor Sanjō says,

> *If in this troubled world*
> *I must linger on*
> *My only friend will be the moon,*
> *Which shines on my sadness,*
> *When other friends are gone.*[25]

But if everyone goes away, it's not enough to say 'That's how it is,' because man's heart demands not to be left alone. Reason is the awareness of reality according to *all* its details; and while the death of

---

[25] Adapted from a translation by William N. Porter.

your friends and your own death are part of reality, the need for happiness and permanence is also a reality in us. A Norwegian poet, the Nobel prize-winner, Pär Lagerkvist, says in one of his poems, 'There is no one who hears when someone cries in the darkness. But why does that cry exist?'[26] The refusal [in the first sentence] leaves the reality of the question [in the second sentence] intact because the [initial] negative statement is not adequate to reality: reality outstrips the negative answer and is greater. The reality of my heart and my capacity to reason, if it is to remain reason, must accept the fact [that the question remains]. Reason cannot be identified with a depression of the heart that says, 'Ah, there's nothing more'–this is psychosis, pathology. Certainly we need courage to affirm the whole of nature as it manifests itself to the heart, in a heart that is educated and reminded, but we'll look at this question later.

What can best help me to understand the heart I have, my human heart? Ask yourselves, please, what is the present rich in? The present is like a nothingness; the richness of the present comes from the past, and this past is called tradition. The cult of the ancestors is one of the grandest and most powerful expressions of humanity. [Today] I read you two passages of your ancient literature–just as I always read passages, ancient and modern, of all the world's literature–and all this reading has advantages. It is if the [authors] had written for *me*, and this shows how tradition illumines the desires of the heart.

A break with tradition, or any break with the past, means to break with your own heart. Who gains by breaking with the past and thereby taking away our memory? There is a great Mexican writer, Octavio Paz, who affirms a basic idea. In 1979, speaking of the Mexican people, he said, and I quote, 'It's become a

---

[26] Pär Lagerkvist, from *Aftonland*, translated by W.H. Auden.

people without memory.' Czeslaw Miloscz, in his 1980
Nobel prize acceptance speech, also warned that the
European people were systematically being 'deprived
of memory.' A people that has lost its memory is an
empty people that is unable to speak to itself, and for
this reason Aleksandr Solzhenitsyn, the greatest
writer of our time, in his 1972 Nobel acceptance
speech, denounced censorship, which results in the
people's 'excision of memory' and eventually gives rise
to 'mute generations.'[27] I remember when I was in
Prague, the capital of Czechoslovakia, for the first
time, ten years ago. I went to eat in the best
restaurant in town, in the Castle, the Great Castle of
Prague. There were only three of us. At eight o'clock
hundreds of young people came in, men and women,
and they filled all the tables, four by four. They
ordered glasses of beer. The place closed at eleven;
we were ashamed to talk because [all around us] a
hundred or so young people stayed there for three
hours, sat in front of glasses of beer without talking;
they had nothing to say. The great wealth of the
present is memory. Who gains by deleting it? In order
to tackle the present you need a criterion, and a
criterion comes to you from the wisdom of the past.
What do we call it when we tackle the present
without a criterion? We use the word, 'reaction,' or
'instinct' [because a person] just reacts, you are just
instinctive [when you give] answers. Who gains if
people act by instinct, or by reaction, and not in the
light of a wise hypothesis? [Those in power benefit

---

[27] "Woe to that nation whose literature is cut short by the intrusion of
force. This is [...] the sealing up of a nation's heart, the excision of its
memory. A nation can no longer remember itself, it loses its spiritual
unity, and despite their seemingly common language, countrymen cease
to understand one another. Mute generations live out their lives and die,
without giving an account of their experiences either to themselves or
to their descendants," from the 1972 Nobel Lecture by Aleksandr
Solzhenitsyn.

when people lose their memory]. Power can be
something great if it is a service. Serving what?
People, persons. But power, when it acts in order to
affirm its own ideology or its own conception of
things, needs people to be as instinctive as possible,
as reactive as possible. Why? Because through the
instruments of influence, in other words through the
mass media and compulsory schooling, it passes on
its ideology. And this slavery or alienation–these are
words that express what happens when a people has
an excision of memory and becomes 'mute'–gives rise
to an alleged 'ideal' of life that is called 'comfort.' In
this way the powers that be seek to please young
people, and the young people settle for this comfort,
but they grow up without hope and with violent
tendencies, because people are made for something
more than mere comfort: we have been made for a
total harmony.

A Reasonable Human Journey How can we
achieve this relationship? This total harmony that we
desire expresses itself, 'speaks' with the 'voice' that is
the heart of the human person, something fragile and
contradictory. How then can we live this total
harmony if it's so mysterious and seems so
contradictory? I believe, because of my experience,
that nothing corresponds more to the soul, not only
of a young person, but of an adult who is fully alive,
than conceiving life as a journey. A reasonable, human
journey has two clear factors. The first one requires a
certainty that life moves toward a final positivity; this
certainty follows from recognizing that nature cries
out for this final perfection. Without the intuition that
all of life progresses toward an ultimate positivity, the
violence of power, whether provisional or not, and
cynicism or inhumanity in practical life would be just.
The second factor involves recognizing the fact that I
have not yet reached this destiny of which I am
certain. Though it remains mysterious because I have

not yet attained it, all my effort strains toward seeking to follow the good suggestions in my existence and pardoning myself the mistakes I make a thousand times a day.

To set out on a journey toward this total harmony that we desire, we must have certainty and an indomitable striving toward an ultimate positivity; these two factors, which make a human journey possible, also constitute morality. What expresses this moral tending toward a final harmony, of which we are certain, even if we have not yet attained this positivity? What characterizes those who, though well aware of their own fragility, never give up? This quality is called entreaty, or begging: begging this destiny, whatever form it may take, to come. Because I have to use a word in order to address this wholeness or harmony, I choose the greatest word that I have: 'you.' You, destiny, whoever you are, I call on you, I beg you. Entreaty prevails as the supreme rational expression. We Christians call it prayer, but the essence of what we call prayer consists in the entreaty that the Mystery come.

The Eternal Value of Even the Smallest Flower
What can help me to maintain this disposition of entreaty, so that my begging prevails over the tendency toward skepticism characteristic of instinctiveness and reactivity? Those who are instinctive or reactive become sceptics, who do not get involved with life, because they can only get involved with what they feel. By contrast, those who experience life as an entreaty to the Mystery—as an entreaty to the Mystery to come, an entreaty to destiny to come—they get involved with everything, even with the smallest detail. This is why Jesus said, 'Even a word said lightly has an eternal value.'[28] He also said that even the smallest flower of the field has

---

[28] See Matthew 12:36.

an eternal value.[29] But I need help to convert my life into an entreaty to the Mystery, so that I don't disappoint myself through letting myself be deluded by the prevailing attitude: a most resolute and comfortable skepticism. I know only one effective aid in this endeavor: a companionship, that is, a friendship among persons who sense this need to beg and who help each other. This is the only true friendship: being together in front of destiny. This should be the meaning of man and of woman: not the illusory falling in love that young people dream of and with which they identify something great, but rather a companionship that walks together on the same road toward a common destiny, that rouses us from our sleep, that calls us back from our distraction, and that doesn't allow us to suffocate in our pettiness or wickedness. The world is like a morning at dawn in which you can turn your back to the sun and say, 'It's all darkness,' or you can choose to turn your back on the darkness and then say, 'The daylight is coming.' This is life; this is the world. Whether you turn your back on the light or look toward the light involves a decision or an option chosen in freedom; but the two alternatives are not equal. You can't choose whatever you like because one of the two alternatives is irrational and unjust. The half-light means that the light is there; therefore if you say, 'It's not bright: so all is darkness,' you betray your own experience and you betray reality. If someone has felt the desire for joy, it's a crime for that person to say that the world is negative. The instant of joy springs up like a fount of entreaty to the infinite. The companionship makes it possible for you to remain true to this instant of joy and supports you in entreaty; thus, the companionship emerges as an essential condition for persons to be themselves. The companionship is like

---

[29] See Matthew 6:29.

41

the soil in which the seed becomes a plant. The companionship does not substitute for the person's development, but it makes this growth possible. This is why those in power hate and fear an integrated, unabridged tradition and always fear those who get together in companionship to walk toward destiny.

Forgive me for speaking of my tradition for a moment, but in my heritage, that voice of the universe, of the whole reality that I spoke of, appears, takes human form, and makes itself heard in the human heart. The news that this voice, this 'wholeness' became man has reached me, in such a way that this Presence can also be my heart's companion, can be present here and now. That the whole, the mystery of the whole, has become human, like me and now keeps me company, so much so that my heart rests on Him, I have to admit–I have to acknowledge–that this is something moving and great. It seems to me to be the greatest hypothesis imaginable. Forgive me for this final witness concerning my own tradition. Let me add that the way to total harmony or wholeness is not important as long as it's a way, traveled together with sincerity of heart.

And thanks for everything. I thank my colleague, who has now become my friend, who has made the great effort to translate for me. Above all, I am moved and filled with admiration for the President and the directors of the International Center because I have never found elsewhere such a great openness."[30]

---

[30] "Clarity of Faith Before Buddhism at its Best," *Traces*, No. 5, 1999.

Not Merely a Visit But the Beginning of a Friendship
At the first meeting, the two men, each noted within his own culture for spiritual acumen, looked at each other in silence and then embraced. It was a heartfelt embrace, like that of friends. Finally, they spoke.

Habukawa would later recall that, "after a short break, we went to visit the Reihokan treasure house," a museum "where, amid the many exhibits, a scroll of the thousand-armed [goddess of Compassion] captured" Giussani's fascination. "I explained the meaning of the thousand arms of Senjyu-kannon Bodhisattva, the numberless ways of saving people from their suffering, and I heard that afterwards Monsignor Giussani always kept a picture of this Bodhisattva."[31]

That evening, Habukawa took Giussani to the University of Koyasan, where the Novice Master was also a professor. Then-University President Dr. Takagi Shingen, the ex-President Dr. Matsunaga Yukei, the attendant, Dr. Riva, and the journalist Roberto Fontolan joined them for an evening of warm dialogue and great openness, during which Professor Habukawa was surprised by how very well-informed Giussani was about the historical facts of Shingon Buddhism's founding and development. Giussani was particularly moved by the emphasis Shingon's founder, Kukai Kobo-Daishi, had placed on education and his requirement that students study both Japanese and foreign works, which was an unusually progressive practice for the time.

Fr. Giussani's interest in the public university that Kukai founded toward the end of the first millennium deeply impressed Professor Habukawa, who later recalled that because this "was the topic discussed during this first encounter with Monsignor

---

[31] Shodo Habukawa, "Monsignor Giussani is a Part of Me," *Traces*, No. 6, 2006.

Giussani, [it] created a common bond between us, giving the feeling of ten years of friendship."[32]

Not merely an enjoyable evening of academic conversation, this meeting generated something new among them: friendships that remain to this day and that traverse the boundaries of land and sea, and indeed the boundaries of life and beyond.

The following year, at Fr. Giussani's invitation, Professor Habukawa journeyed to Italy and spoke at the Rimini Meeting, the first of his many appearances at the annual week-long gathering. "I recited an old proverb as a metaphor for our cultural exchange: 'When the butterfly comes, the flower opens; when the flower opens, the butterfly comes.' I used this citation for the occasion of the cultural encounter between Christianity and its Christian culture and Buddhism and the Shingon Buddhist culture. I expressed our happiness for having started a friendship between the people of Italy and Japan."[33]

Samuele Rosa, a member of the receiving delegation that greeted Habukawa during a 1991 trip to Milan, showed Habukawa and a small group of Koyasan novices around northern Italy, including Milan, Como, and the Alps. "Throughout all those days," Rosa said, "you could definitely see that they were touched by the friendship with Giussani," who joined them for a festive dinner. They were visibly moved "by his interest in their culture, in their lives." Rosa noted that though this reunion took place four years after their initial introduction to Fr. Giussani and the Movement, "I was struck by how clearly visible on their faces was the sense of the privilege and total love with which Giussani had embraced them, as if it had happened yesterday. It made you think, Have I been as grateful for what I have met?"

---

32 *Ibid.*

33 *Ibid.*

Rosa asked one of the monks what he liked best about Italy. Wakako Saito, Habukawa's indefatigable translator, posed the question in Japanese. The monk replied, "The traditional songs from Naples, especially 'Torna a Sorriento.'" Surprised, Rosa asked, "Why do you like those songs?" The monk paused for a moment, deep in thought. Then he uttered a single word: "Nostalgia."

Fascinated yet puzzled, Rosa pressed further. "What does that mean for you?" The monk retreated into silent thought once more. Then he said, "The longing for an absent good." This understanding, Rosa maintains, is one of the fruits of the monks' friendship with Giussani. Professor Habukawa is renowned for his great dignity and silence; Rosa understood his silence as "a constant quest for the Almighty. Habukawa has a look *full* of the quest for the Almighty." Rosa contends that in Habukawa's tradition, "he finds Giussani the best ally in this quest."

Putting your life in front of the Mystery makes your life more vibrant and warm, Rosa said, and "this is how Giussani took the original quest for the Almighty and made it a quest for life."[34]

On February 23, 2005, Shodo Habukawa received the unexpected, and deeply saddening news of Fr. Giussani's death; but in neither Buddhism nor Christianity is death the final arbiter of friendship. "Since that message arrived," Habukawa said a year later, "I always keep a photo of Monsignor Giussani

---

[34] Samuele Rosa, Interview with Mark Danner, August 9, 2018.

with me to pray that he advise me on the way. I'm praying that our relationship remains eternal."[35]

---

[35] Shodo Habukawa, "Monsignor Giussani is a Part of Me," *Traces*, No. 6, 2006.

TOMOKO SADAHIRO: THE HEART IS ALWAYS THE SAME

"The emotion of friendship is amongst the most mighty and the most mysterious of human instincts."
— Robert Hugh Benson

A striking fact demonstrates Christianity's tumultuous history in Japan: each and every canonized Japanese saint is a martyr. This history began on August 15, 1549, when the Jesuits Francis Xavier, Cosme de Torres, and Juan Fernández arrived in Kagoshima, Japan. They'd journeyed from Spain with hopes of sharing the faith, and, at least initially, the signs were promising. Xavier visited Shimazu Takahisa, the *daimyō* (or feudal lord) of Kagoshima, and asked for permission to build the first Catholic mission in the country. The *daimyō* said yes, although not necessarily for altruistic reasons: he hoped to create a trade relationship with Europe.

The imperial government and shogunate were, at first, kindly disposed towards the missionaries, seeing in them a way to undermine the power wielded by Buddhist monks, who had the respect of the people. Over time, however, the government increasingly viewed Christians with suspicion, believing them pawns in a much larger colonialist enterprise. They banned Catholicism and gruesomely executed those Japanese unwilling to renounce the new faith.

Today there is no threat of a violent backlash against Christians in Japan, but sharing Christ nevertheless meets obstacles caused by a lingering sense among many Japanese that they already know what Christianity is: something peculiar to the West and ultimately alien to their culture. Encounters still happen, though, because the needs of the heart remain the same the world over.

Tomoko Sadahiro—her friends call her Sako—lives in Hiroshima and is part of Japan's small Communion and Liberation (CL)[36] community.

"If I think back over the story of the past decades, I realize that God truly wanted me; He wanted me to be here. He literally pulled me! I remember that I had had some problems with some friends of mine, and afterwards I discovered in myself the desire for something more, and I said, 'I want something that doesn't end.'"

Not long after, she encountered an Italian—Angela—who introduced Sako to CL. "Even though I wasn't Christian, I attended the Jesuit Catholic University, where among other subjects I studied Gregorian chant, so it was obligatory for me to participate in a few masses, like Christmas and Easter." Her friendship with Angela and Angela's

---

[36] The lay Catholic movement founded by Luigi Giussani.

husband grew, and in time she began preparation for baptism, which she received in 1985.

Traces, the official magazine of CL, is published in multiple languages around the world, and remains one of the Movement's most effective means of introducing people to the charism of Fr. Giussani. Following her baptism, Sako began translating issues of Tracce–the Italian-language edition–into Japanese.

"There are two of us translating Traces, myself and Marcia, a Japanese-Brazilian woman. During the day, I work in the archbishop's office. In the evening when we get home, we do the translation. It takes a lot of time, about two or three months per issue, because there are many difficulties with some concepts or some words. For example, the concept of 'identity' is not part of the common language, and is only found in academic contexts, so we simply use the English word. Or the word 'charity'–it doesn't exist in Japanese. It's the same for other words. In the end, we manage to do about three issues a year.

"We send Traces to all the bishops, monks, and superiors of congregations," she continued. "Over two hundred copies were sent last year. We're not slaves to 'results,' but if someone reads it and responds, or if something happens because of our work, this encourages us greatly!"

Christianity is a companionship Sako likes to recount a story in which her work for Traces played an unexpected role in a friend's happiness.

"I have a friend who left CL ten years ago because she said it didn't correspond to her. Three years ago, she had a grave problem. She sought me out and we began doing charitable work together, taking food to homeless men who live in the city. After the charitable work, we often spoke in the car and she would ask me lots of questions. This went on for three years. I always insisted on what Fr. Giussani had taught me, something that has always stayed with me: look attentively at reality, because reality calls you to the Mystery.

My friend and I even argued a couple of times, something rare in Japan, because in general we keep everything inside, including our irritation. In one issue of *Traces*, we had published the translation of the summary of the booklet called *Something Within Something*. She read it, and continued reading it every day, until finally shc said, 'Sako, I finally understand what Fr. Giussani is saying!' She was elated! And I was, too. In the end, she expressed her desire to resume the relationship with us."

Sako concluded, "The heart is always the same, everywhere."[37]

Japanese Kanji Character for the word, kokoro,
Meaning "heart, mind, spirit"

---

[37] Paolo Perego, "Leafing Through *Traces* in Japanese," *Traces*, No.9, 2006.

MARK DANNER: THE URGENCY OF CIRCUMSTANCE

"It is not for the stone to choose its place."[38]

"I have a surprise to announce!" my mother exclaimed as I arrived home from school one day in early 1976. In my wildest dreams as a fourteen-year-old I could not have imagined what she was about to tell me, nor the consequences it would have for my life.

"You are going to skip a year of school and travel around the world, because your father has been invited to join two other professors and twenty American college students to encounter and study the world's great non-Judeo-Christian religions." What I felt was the excitement of skipping my eighth-grade year and exploring the world—Morocco,

---

[38] Paul Claudel, *The Tidings Brought to Mary*, (Chicago: Gateway, 1960), 14.

Jerusalem, Iran (on the eve of the revolution), India, Sri Lanka, Hong Kong, and Japan. I couldn't yet understand that the geographic expanse my family would traverse in 1976 and 1977 would serve only as a doorway to the infinite vistas that would open in my heart and soul, most particularly through my encounter with Buddhism in its many diverse expressions.

This year of adventure and discovery, marked by encounters with humble men and women of deepest piety and wisdom, set my religious sense on fire. The hearts of these people radiated a love that made me feel like I had always known them. Some were simple Tibetan Buddhist monks, others were Sufi mystics. One was the renowned Bengali sage Sri Anandamayi Ma, arguably one of the greatest female figures in the history of India, and perhaps even in twentieth century world history, though she is almost completely unknown in the West. I also became friends with America's greatest scholar of comparative religion, Huston Smith, one of the three professors on this voyage of the soul. Huston's renown never awed me, because he always behaved in the most gentle, curious, and joyful way I'd ever seen. He was the first adult who treated me as his friend, and we remained friends throughout the years.

When I was a baby, my French mother and American father had brought me to be baptized a Catholic while we all lived in Morocco. But due to my father's opposition and to particularly difficult religious circumstances in the family, I grew up without ever going to church, except during annual summer visits to my maternal grandparents' home in France, where my mother, brother, and I would visit while my father would stay in Bloomington, Indiana, to teach summer university classes.

India As winter approached, I met my first Buddhists in northern India, where they lived as refugees from Tibet, a country invaded by communist China in 1950. As a young boy I had grown up hearing and reading the stories of persecuted Russians in the USSR, and I had voraciously read stories by survivors of the Nazi *Shoah*.

Yet the story of the Tibetan cultural genocide by the Chinese army seized me in a different way, not only because the Chinese had committed atrocities against such a peaceful people, but particularly because of the way that the Tibetans (some of whom I had met) responded to having been forced to flee their homeland. Though homesick for sure, not one expressed bitterness or hatred toward the Chinese.

This first encounter with a people who embodied mercy and gentleness of heart provoked me to ask myself, "In the face of unspeakable personal suffering and trauma, where does such a compassionate human heart spring from? And why did these Tibetans embrace their faith as a total way of life?"

While living in the ancient city of Varanasi (Benares), spread along the banks of the Ganges River, our family, the students, and their professors would take day trips into the surrounding region. One of these trips brought us to Bodhgaya, a sacred site for Buddhists because they believe that in that place, young Gautama Buddha attained complete self-awareness and awareness of the central truths of life.

I don't remember much about our time there, but I will never forget one "chance" encounter with a young Tibetan monk, dressed in his maroon robe. One of the students on the trip, Walter, had become both my martial arts instructor and my friend, and he and I were in a restaurant eating delicious *momos*, or meat dumplings, when I remember seeing the monk. His smile and gentleness were infectious. In fact, his presence made a greater impression on me than the famous ruins and ancients temples of this holy town.

Afterward, with my curiosity piqued, I bought a number of books on Buddhism and got to work studying this religion and its teachings, in an attempt to grasp what had so inspired its Tibetan followers. I wanted to know everything about Tibet. I devoured picture books by explorers of the early twentieth century: Sven Hedin of Sweden; Giussepe Tucci of Italy; and of course the famous Alexandra David-Neel of France, who disguised herself as a Buddhist pilgrim to pass into a land closed off to foreigners.

The vistas of the vast Tibetan plateaus and high-altitude lakes, dominated by the towering and snow-capped Himalayan Mountains, enchanted me.

At the base of these mystical mountains, the photos revealed hundreds of Tibet's ancient Buddhist monasteries, where both celibate men and women lived in prayer and devotion. From these books, I learned that some monasteries were so expansive, they spread to the size of cities and that traditionally, Tibetan families sent their firstborn sons to the monasteries; but after the Chinese army's atrocities, huge numbers of monks and faithful, led by their religious leader the Dalai Lama, sought refuge across the Himalayas in northern India.

Imagine my delight, then, when Walter asked my parents if I could join him during the Christmas break for a road trip into the foothills of the Himalayas, to the mountain city of Darjeeling, famed for its sloped tea estates and home to numerous Tibetan monasteries.

The Monastery With the parental green light, we set off from Varanasi's bustling railway station, filled with tea vendors and morning passengers brushing their teeth with small Neem tree sticks.

Suddenly, in the midst of the crowds, we experienced another "chance" encounter: we recognized the very same Tibetan monk that we had met in Bodhgaya! He was on his way to visit his parents' small farm in the hills below Darjeeling, and expressed great joy when we invited him to become our traveling companion.

As our open-sided pickup bus began its ascent on the winding roads to Darjeeling—a former hill station frequented by British colonists during the baking summer heat that envelops the Gangetic Plain during the monsoon season—the winter mists chilled my bones. I laughed at the comical road signs warning drivers to exercise caution. My favorite was, "If you drive like hell, you'll soon get there!" When we had arrived in our monk friend's village, he asked the bus driver to stop, and we hopped off and headed down a trail to meet his parents in their little house. We then caught the next bus going by and headed towards our evening destination, a Tibetan Buddhist monastery that hosted us for the night. I couldn't contain my curiosity as all of sudden what had been only photos and text became reality before my eyes.

As we settled, hungry and tired from the journey, into our little room lined with books, we heard a knock on our door. When we answered it, a monk invited us to attend that evening's services in the main hall. We gladly accepted and arrived as the monks were chanting. Their deep-throated voices offered prayers that were so unlike anything I'd ever heard that I was initially put off—this was nothing like Gregorian chant!

In fact, Huston Smith later introduced the West to this form of prayer through recordings he'd made of the unique and eerie phenomenon of Tibetan monastic chanting, which at times is done in simultaneous tones by a single voice.

The mystery of the moment captivated me: surrounded by sights, sounds, and smells that were so "other," I was amazed my friend could compose himself enough to close his eyes in meditation. As the chants ended, I had to nudge him gently with my elbow when two monks came by with bowls, spoons, and a bucket of steaming porridge. It was dinner time.

I devoured my food and was surprised to see the serving monks come by for a second round. I accepted, and respectfully finished off a second bowl. Assuming that I must have been starving, the monks came by for a third round, but at this point I declared surrender. As we departed the next morning, one of our hosts generously insisted that I "borrow" an English-language book of photos and text on Tibet's Buddhist history. I promised to bring it back someday.

Waiting for our bus at the monastery's gates I was struck by the little boys who were novice monks, playing around as all boys do, but these were dressed in robes and sandals. Didn't they miss their families? Did they realize the life that was before them? Were they happy in this community? This had been my first encounter with monasticism and there was something very deep and profound in the lives of these men, something that I briefly shared. There was something majestic about their ascetical lives devoted to a faith that was 400 years older than Christianity– something as sweeping as the vistas of the snowcapped Himalayas we subsequently enjoyed when the fog enshrouding the hills of Darjeeling briefly lifted.

Warmer Climes Weeks later, I found myself pouring over my books on Buddhism with renewed enthusiasm, this time from the palm tree-lined beaches of the island of Sri Lanka, whose majority Sinhalese ethnic community practiced a different school of Buddhist teaching.

Again, I was touched by the witness of the monks in their orange robes, chanting next to a large statue of this mysterious man of divine-like stature, the Buddha. This was a particularly solemn moment that I was witnessing, as the recently-completed statue of the Buddha was being painted with a third "eye"– symbolizing enlightenment.

I marveled at the abbot in charge who described to us his life as a monk and how through a lifetime of meditation he only needed two hours of sleep a night.

His story recalled what Huston told us about Tibetan monks whose mastery over their mind allowed them to generate enough body heat to dry wet blankets draped over their shoulders on a cold day. Mind over matter, yes; detachment from the world, yes–but were they happy? This was a question that pushed forward in my heart when I encountered such devotion and faith, the likes of which I had never seen in America.

Rising Sun As my year of adventure drew to a close, I spent the last seven weeks of our voyage enraptured by the stoic and ordered beauty of Buddhist Japan.

We were based in the ancient city of Kyoto, where spring had arrived and the cherry tree blossoms framed the gravel walkways leading to some of the world's most exquisite temples. As the family photographer, I was in paradise, capturing on film the temple moss and rock gardens where every plant, rock, pool, or lake was placed as a reflection of a thirst for infinite beauty, a foretaste of total bliss.

I was so curious about this unusual country, in which a thousand-year-old temple, seemingly untouched by the centuries, could stand sandwiched between towering modern buildings and be ringed by the hustle and bustle of urban life. I wanted to know what these temples and sacred spaces meant to the Japanese people. Were they mere national treasures of a grand heritage? Or were they gateways into the Mystery, where men and women could seek repose of the heart and inner peace?

I was able to glimpse again, as I had at the Tibetan monastery, the moving witness of men plunged into a relentless search to know themselves and discover the meaning of life: we were invited to spend the day in meditation with the monks of a Buddhist monastery on Mt. Hiei, not far from Kyoto.

I recall the silence of the towering cedar and pine trees, and the silence of the monks—not to mention the shooting pain I experienced when trying to move my legs after sitting cross-legged on tatami straw mats for extended periods of time.

The monks invited us to share their simple meal of steamed rice, pickles, and other vegetables. I had read that the monks made sure to eat the last grain of rice on their plate, so I forced myself to eat every last bite of the strange-tasting fare. I soon discovered, to my extreme embarrassment, that my younger brother had found the food so unappetizing that he had hardly touched his tray.

An Enkindled Religious Sense I was not the same when I returned to my hometown early that summer. Indeed, I can say that this trip around the world was the point at which my "religious sense"—to use the expression of Fr. Giussani—was kindled into a roaring fire. I had seen, tasted, smelled, and experienced what man's search for total meaning had generated across the centuries: yearnings etched in sublime temples and sculptures; wisdom distilled into vast libraries of esoteric texts written in some of the oldest languages known to mankind; and of a way of being in the world yet free of attachments to "things"—including the rage that boils up in a person's heart when their homeland is pillaged and burned, as the Tibetan nation had experienced at the hands of the Chinese government.

I had contemplated statues and paintings of this "realized" man, Gautama Buddha, who for Buddhists was a living consciousness into which one could be united.

I had traipsed across the world with Huston Smith, whose child-like smile, so full of wonder and curiosity, had filled me with a desire to live like him. So much so, in fact, that through the years of only indirect contact and occasional news, I regularly prayed that God grant me the grace to know the very moment Huston died: I wanted to ask that his laughter in heaven bless me.[39]

The Thirst for the Real, the Urgency of Circumstance What my encounter with Buddhism provoked in me was a thirst for what is real, for what really matters in life—and that was certainly not, I thought, something I could find in my Midwestern high school, where classmates did not have the slightest interest in hearing where I had been for the past year.

I prayed and meditated all by myself—sharing nothing of my heart with anyone.

I was waiting for something—or someone—to come. And He came, in the here and now, through the reality of my life—not in a nostalgic memory of my mystical voyage. He came in the suffering, tears, new friendships, and joys of my life as a graduate college student, who saw not only my family disintegrate but also saw my mother's Catholic faith blossom with mercy and forgiveness toward my father.

I befriended Christian Maronites escaping the bloody civil war in Lebanon, who arrived in America with stories of terror and tragedy but who were also forgiving and free of hatred.

During a college semester abroad, I met a Dominican monk in Jerusalem on whose shoulders I

---

[39] In an extraordinary coincidence, on December 31, 2016, I happened to speak to someone I rarely contacted, and was stunned when she told me that Kendra, Huston's wife, had called her the night before to announce that Huston had died that day.

cried over the latest tragedies and massacres in Lebanon—and he never asked me if I believed in Jesus.

In college I met Evangelical Protestant students who became my best friends, including one who became my roommate for four years. His love of the Lord moved me to open the Bible again and begin reading with the same questions that had stirred me when reading the esoteric Buddhist and Hindu texts only a few years before.

Answers came in the faces of new friends and experiences. The first church meeting I ever attended on my own was a Quaker Protestant service—whose announced theme, "The Evidence of Lives Changed," would encapsulate the motivation for every step I took in my return to the faith of my baptism.

For it was thanks to my encounter with Buddhism and all the little "Buddhas" along my path— such as Huston Smith—that my eyes were opened to recognize Christ when He beckoned in the immediacy and urgency of my circumstances.

Back...But Still Searching I came back to the Church in my second year of college, quite alone as a Catholic college student, but very much at home with my Protestant friends. It was a moving experience to finally attend mass with Mom, who had never once chastised me for not going with her in the years after dad left her.

Later, while pursuing a Master's Degree in Arab Studies at Georgetown University, my heart remained unsatisfied with the Catholicism that I had encountered, characterized by the combative stance of student activists engaged in the culture wars of that time. I was restless and thirsty for a Presence, and tired of fighting for "Christian values."

Then, as years before when my mother had announced we would travel the world, a decisive event occurred.

At a boring weekend party, a Presence arrived through the words of a friend. I wish I could remember the precise words he used, but it went something like, "Hey, there's this group of Italians and American Catholics who meet every week...they're part of this group called Communion and Liberation..."

I'm not sure why–perhaps it was a prompting of the Holy Spirit–but instantly I was certain that these were people I had to meet.

A *Companionship Open to the Other* From the moment a smiling Dr. Mauro Ceroni opened the door and invited me in for dinner, I walked into a friendship that embraced me with a delightful simplicity and joy.

Years later, having eventually married one of my first friends in CL, I had the opportunity to travel to Berkeley, California, on a business trip. This was before Huston Smith had passed away, so I grabbed the opportunity to pay a call on him and his wife, Kendra, and was joined by my old friend Walter (with whom I had gone to Darjeeling).

Huston's sparkling eyes and lovely, lilting voice pried me with questions about my life. He was especially fascinated by my encounter with Fr. Giussani. He wanted to know all about Giussani's idea of the "religious sense." I babbled on enthusiastically, only later realizing to my utter shame that I had done most of the talking, while this old man, hard of hearing but possessing a little boy's heart, smiled as if discovering a new wonder. In one of his last books, Huston cited Giussani, a small consolation for a missed opportunity to sit at the feet of my first "spiritual father."

Today I live in the Maryland countryside, a fifteen minute car ride from the Xa Loi Buddhist temple, built in a transformed barn.

I met its small Vietnamese abbot, Thich Bao
Thanh, on a cold autumn day as he strolled the
temple's long driveway. A warm friendship developed
between us, and eventually Master Mai Li—as he is
called by his martial arts students—agreed to
introduce me to Vietnam's unique fighting style. I was
amazed by his litheness, and by his powerful and
beautiful movements as he demonstrated for me.

When I asked him how Buddhists like himself,
those who believe in non-violence, could justify
practicing and teaching a fighting art, he smiled and
explained that his purpose was not to destroy an
enemy, but rather to take a man down so he can have
the opportunity to reflect on his life, repent, and
begin a new way of living.

As I got to know Mai Li he told me the story of
his life. I was surprised to learn that he had grown up
in a Catholic family but had left the faith. He studied
martial arts with a grandmaster who took him under
his wing. When I consider the choice that Mai Li
made, it is easy for me to avoid judging him, for I need
only look at my own life and at how Christ
mysteriously drew me to Him through the Buddha.

Now, as a son of Fr. Giussani, I experience a deep
sense of unity with Mai Li, and a sense of peace as I
pray my rosary while walking around the temple's
beautiful lake, or sit in its silent prayer hall,
expressing gratitude to Our Lady for all the graces
that her Son has given me.

EPILOGUE: WHEN THE BUTTERFLY ARRIVES

"Working together is a sacramental fact."
— *Massimo Camisasca*

We live in fractious times.

Humanity has always been riven by disputes and disagreements, hostilities and misunderstandings. But our own historical era appears unusually torn, exhibiting a disappointing skepticism of the "other," the different. People retreat into ideologies and merely talk past each other—when they're not actually shouting and calling each other names. And too often, religion is cited as justification for such antipathy.

Fr. Luigi Giussani offers a novel yet thoroughly Christian approach to the problem: attention to the heart's original needs, which are the same in every human being. "For Giussani," says Fr. José Medina, national leader for CL in the United States, "the 'heart,' far from being a collection of subjective emotions, is the innate and universal longing for truth, beauty, justice and good, ultimately God."[40] This insight generates a fascination for the other and a genuine openness to him or her, for they are no longer alien or unapproachably different—they are human.

Giussani's unexpected 1987 encounter with Shodo Habukawa—and the friendship it generated—provides an example of this truth in action.

"Unrestricted openness, the characteristic of dialogue considered as a factor in the development of a person and in the creation of a new society, has one extremely important condition: dialogue requires that I be conscious of who I am. A dialogue is genuine only if it is lived as a comparison between the other's proposal and the awareness of the proposal I offer, the proposal I am; otherwise it is not a dialogue. To express it in a different way, it is a dialogue only insofar as I'm aware of myself and my maturity. For this reason, unless a crisis—the commitment to sift and sort out tradition—precedes my dialogue with the other, I will remain blocked by the other person's influence or my rejection of the other will make my position unreasonably rigid. Therefore, it is true that a dialogue implies openness toward the other no matter who he is, because he will always introduce an interest, experience, or aspect that otherwise I would have failed to notice. So, in all cases, he leads me to more complete comparisons. A dialogue, nevertheless, also requires maturity on my part and a critical awareness of what I am. Unless we consider this factor, we run the serious risk of confusing dialogue with compromise. To take as a point of

---

[40] José Medina, "Educating the Heart of Man, Just As God Made It," *Humanum*, No. 1, 2015.

departure what we have in common with the other does not necessarily mean that we say the same things as the other, although we may use the same words. For example, the other's conception of justice may not be the Christian conception of justice, or the other's conception of freedom may not be Christian freedom, or the other's conception of education may not be education as the Church understands it. [...] What we do have in common with the other can be found not so much in his ideas as in his innate structure, in those human needs and original standards that make the other a human being just like me."[41]

[41] Luigi Giussani, *The Risk of Education* (New York: Crossroad Publishing Company, 2001), 95.

 PPENDIX

POPE BENEDICT XVI CONCERNING INTERFAITH DIALOGUE

Pope Benedict XVI's Reflections on the 20th Anniversary of Saint John Paul II's Interreligious Prayer Meeting in Assisi, Italy (excerpt)

... John Paul II's [initiative,] promoted 20 years ago, has acquired the features of an accurate prophecy. His invitation to the world's religious leaders to bear a unanimous witness to peace serves to explain with no possibility of confusion that religion must be a herald of peace.

As the Second Vatican Council taught in the Declaration *Nostra Aetate* on the Relation of the Church to Non-Christian Religions: "We cannot truly pray to God the Father of all if we treat any people in other than brotherly fashion, for all men are created in God's image" (n. 5).

Despite the differences that mark the various religious itineraries, recognition of God's existence, which human beings can only arrive at by starting from the experience of creation (cf. Rom 1:20), must dispose believers to view other human beings as brothers and sisters. It is not legitimate, therefore, for anyone to espouse religious difference as a presupposition or pretext for an aggressive attitude towards other human beings.

It could be objected that history has experienced the regrettable phenomenon of religious wars. We know, however, that such demonstrations of violence cannot be attributed to religion as such but to the cultural limitations with which it is lived and develops in time.

Yet, when the religious sense reaches maturity it gives rise to a perception in the believer that faith in God, Creator of the universe and Father of all, must encourage relations of universal brotherhood among human beings.

In fact, attestations of the close bond that exists between the relationship with God and the ethics of love are recorded in all great religious traditions. We Christians feel strengthened in this and further enlightened by the Word of God. The Old Testament already expresses God's love for all peoples which, in the covenant that he established with Noah, he gathered in one great embrace, symbolized by the "bow in the clouds" (Gn 9:13, 14, 16), and which, according to the Prophets' words, he intended to gather once and for all into a single universal family (cf. Is 2:2ff.; 42:6; 66:18-21; Jer 4:2; Ps 47[46]).

In the New Testament the revelation of this universal plan of love culminates in the Paschal Mystery, in which the Son of God Incarnate, in an overwhelming act of saving solidarity, offers himself as a sacrifice on the Cross for the whole of humanity. *Thus, God demonstrates that his nature is Love*. This is what I meant to emphasize in my first Encyclical, which begins precisely with the words "*Deus caritas est*" (I Jn 4:7).

Scripture's assertion not only casts light on God's mystery but also illumines relations between human beings who are called to abide by the commandment of love.

The gathering that St. John Paul II organized in Assisi appropriately puts the emphasis on the *value of prayer in building peace*. Indeed, we are aware of how difficult and, at times, how humanly desperate this process can be. Peace is a value in which so many elements converge. To build it, the paths of cultural, political and economic order are, of course, important, but first of all *peace must be built in hearts*. It is here, in fact, that sentiments develop that can nurture it or, on the contrary, threaten, weaken and stifle it.

Moreover, the human heart is the place where God intervenes. In this regard, in addition to the "horizontal" dimension of relations with other human beings, the "vertical" dimension of each person's relationship with God, the foundation of all things, is proving to be of fundamental importance. This was exactly what Pope John Paul II intended to recall to the world with the 1986 event.

He asked for genuine prayer which involves the whole of life. Thus, he desired it to be accompanied by fasting and expressed in pilgrimage, a symbol of the journey towards the encounter with God. And he explained, "Prayer entails conversion of heart on our part" (*Inauguration of the World Day of Prayer for Peace*, Assisi, 27 October 1986, n. 4; *L'Osservatore Romano* English edition, 3 November, p. 1).

Among the features of the 1986 Meeting, it should be stressed that this value of prayer in building peace *was testified to by the representatives of different religious traditions*, and this did not happen at a distance but *in the context of a meeting*. Consequently, the people of diverse religions who were praying could show through the language of witness that prayer does not divide but unites and is a decisive element for an effective pedagogy of peace, hinged on friendship, reciprocal acceptance and dialogue between people of different cultures and religions.

We are in greater need of this dialogue than ever, especially if we look at the new generations. Sentiments of hatred and vengeance have been inculcated in numerous young people in those parts of the world marked by conflicts, in ideological contexts where the seeds of ancient resentment are cultivated and their souls prepared for future violence. These barriers must be torn down and encounter must be encouraged...[42]

---

[42] Pope Benedict XVI, L'Osservatore Romano, Weekly Edition in English, 13 September 2006, page 3.

ABOUT THE AUTHORS

Mark Danner is an international business consultant who is passionate about exploring interfaith encounters

Joshua Stancil is a writer and public speaker. He blogs at patheos.com

KathyPeda
206 Foundation Colleen

556744217

10 Jul 2017

Charles Boyd

Linda Enos   British
Humanist

Ment →

8.9   tour, talk

9³⁰ ?   net h/o

max # people – caregivers
              administered
                   resident

Made in the USA
Middletown, DE
18 September 2018